Published by Harrison Metal Press
PO Box 13529
Jackson, Wyoming 83002
United States of America

ISBN 978-1-7372372-2-8

Written by Grasshopper Harrison.

Cover art and illustrations by Frank Grosz.

Printed in the United States of America.

CAPITALI$T BABY

BY
GRASSHOPPER
HARRISON

WITH
ILLUSTRATIONS
BY FRANK
GROSZ

For Charlie Bannon, with gratitude for the hard work.

-- G.H.

And for George Grosz, a constant inspiration.

--F.G.

 is for-

Accountable - personally responsible for your decisions.

Aplomb - calm confidence in tough situations.

Assets - anything we own and use to make our product or service; listed on the left side of a balance sheet.

"Capitalist Baby is accountable for his or her own life, tackling each day with aplomb and using the assets at hand to do great work."

 is for-

Balance sheet - a two-sided snap-shot of all the money tied up in a business; one side shows where it all came from (capital), the other side shows the forms we hold it in (assets).

Bet - a prediction about future outcomes
often made with money.

Budget - a limit on what we can afford to spend.

"Capitalist Baby makes bets on the future,
guided by a budget and a balance sheet."

 is for-

Capital- money we invest to make more money.

Cash- money we use to pay for things day to day.

Cost - how much money it takes to do work, to make a product or service.

"Capitalist Baby raises capital from investors, carefully manages the company's cash, controlling costs of the business."

 is for-

Delaware - a U.S. state where many corporations are created; a special state with a long history of clear and well-respected laws about business.

Director - a member of the governing body of a company, the Board of Directors.

Duty - an obligation to others, as in fiduciary duty or duty of care to stockholders.

"Capitalist Baby values directors on the board who honor their fiduciary duty to stockholders as Delaware law requires."

 is for-

Employee - a person who works at a company, exchanging their output for compensation on terms mutually agreed.

Entrepreneur - a person who starts a business, taking on the risks of failure in exchange for the potential gains of success.

Equity - an ownership stake in a business usually represented by shares of company stock.

"Capitalist Baby hires employees who support her entrepreneurial vision and who are motivated by future gains from equity in the company."

 is for-

Finance - the activities related to money flowing into, around, and out of a company.

Fiduciary - a person who puts stockholders' interests in financial returns ahead of their own personal gain, status, or comfort when making decisions.

Fair-dealing - honest behavior expected of people and companies we do business with; assumption underneath our contracts.

"Capitalist Baby knows finance: cash is life, growth eats cash, cash comes from debt, equity, or operations. And she knows being a fair-dealing fiduciary makes that cash cycle possible."

 is for-

Good Faith - another assumption underneath our contracts: that business partners intend to do the things they say they will do.

Gains - the increase in wealth to both sides that comes from mutually beneficial contracts and trade.

Gross Margin - sales revenue from selling a product minus the variable costs of making it; price minus ingredient costs.

"Capitalist Baby is a good-faith partner to colleagues. Gains from trade with customers increase as gross margin goes up."

 is for-

Higher - a level or amount above the current state.

Hiring - making a job offer to a candidate who agrees to trade their time andwork for money or other compensation.

History - the study of the past to understand how the world changes over time.

"Capitalist Baby knows higher output comes from hiring talented employees to the company. History teaches the do's and don'ts!"

 is for-

Income - the money profit left over after you sell the products and pay the bills.

Incorporation - a special legal form of organization that holds assets, undertakes commercial activities, collects sales and profits, and bears the risks of being in business.

Invest - to purchase assets or finance activities in hopes of future financial returns.

"Capitalist Baby wants more income. The liability shield of incorporation lets him make bold investments to get there."

 is for-

Joy - a feeling of extreme happiness combined with excitement.

Just exchange - a mutually beneficial trade between business colleagues.

"Capitalist Baby finds joy in just exchange in business."

 is for-

Key - critical or most important, as in key performance measure or key person.

Knowledge - facts and ideas – acquired through experience and studying – which help you succeed at work and in life.

"Capitalist Baby seeks out new knowledge to make the best decisions. Meeting and beating key goals is easier when you are curious to learn more."

 is for-

Ladder - figuratively, a way to climb from a lower socio-economic position to a higher one.

Liquidity - cash you can easily move around and exchange for practically anything.

Love - a feeling of warm affection for and devotion to another being, place, thing, or idea.

"Capitalist Baby climbs the ladder of success. Liquidity pays the bills and love for the work does the rest!"

 is for-

Market - a place or mechanism for buyers and sellers to meet and transact.

Management - the practice of coordinating output of a team across business functions.

Mindful - aware of the situation and circumstances around you.

"Capitalist Baby is mindful that good management makes markets more efficient."

 is for-

Net Income - The amount of money left over after all relevant expenses have been subtracted from revenue; aka bottom line on an Income Statement.

Net Present Value - the "today" dollar value of an investment after carefully counting its relevant costs and benefits.

"Capitalist Baby pay attention to Net Income, of course. But she also knows the net present value of the investments she's making in the future."

 is for-

Ownership - a legal claim, typically represented by a share of stock, in the future value of a company or a financial asset.

Objectivity - a focus on the true facts of a situation, represented by evidence.

"Capitalist Baby focuses on facts and evidence. Objectivity increases the value of everyone's ownership in the company."

 is for-

Product - the item or service the company sells to customers; the unit of value which the customer pays for.

Productivity - output per unit of input.

Profit & Loss ("P&L") - aka Income Statement; the financial statement that measures the flow of accounting revenue and expenses, profits or losses, in a business.

"Capitalist Baby knows product quality is key to customer happiness. She carefully measures the team's productivity to ensure a healthy P&L."

 is for-

Question - a request for information to understand what's going on and what might be done about it.

Quantitative reasoning - using numbers or number-based observations to understand a situation and formulate a plan of action.

Qualitative reasoning - using descriptive, rather than number-based, information to understand what's going on and what we might do about it.

"Capitalist Baby is unafraid to ask hard questions. Analyzing tricky situations requires both quantitative and qualitative reasoning."

 is for-

Reality - the state of the world as it is, not as we wish it were.

Risk - the probability of a disappointing outcome.

Retained earnings - the portion of equity capital that comes from operating the business successfully.

"Capitalist Baby understands reality: investor capital and debt are finite. So she takes on risk in order to finance growth from retained earnings."

 is for-

Self-Reliance - independent spirit, taking ownership over your own life.

Special - exceptional or singular due to a unique combination of traits or aptitudes.

Spine - figuratively, strong principles and values that prompt you to "stand up" for what you care about even when you are afraid.

"Capitalist Baby's self-reliance defines her special approach to getting things done. She has confidence and a 'spine' to face adversaries and tricky situations head-on."

 is for-

Trade - mutually beneficial, voluntary transaction between two or more parties.

Talent - skill or aptitude that permits an individual to excel and is unevenly distributed in a population.

Tax - mandatory payment to the government used to fund state spending.

"Capitalist Baby's track record testifies to the power of free trade and low tax rates to spur growth and employment for talented colleagues."

 is for-

Underdog - nickname for the smaller,
new kid on the block in a market.

Upend - transform, often through innovation
in technology or distribution or both.

*"Capitalist Baby is an underdog – the big dogs and
yesterday's winners aren't rooting for Baby – as she
upends the market with new products."*

 is for-

Value - the benefit a customer enjoys from using a product or service, typically higher than the price.

Victory - a triumph over or destruction of competitors; accomplishment of an important goal.

"Capitalist Baby is obsessed with delivering value to her customers. This ensures victory for the business."

 is for-

Work Ethic - commitment of time and effort to deliver output that helps colleagues and customers reach a shared goal.

World View - a mental model of how humans and nature coexist that enables making sense of events and making decisions about one's actions.

"Capitalist Baby's work ethic and world view go hand in hand: if you work hard, Baby believes, you can achieve your goals."

 is for-

"X" marks the spot - where the parties sign contracts in a mutually beneficial exchange of money, resources, know-how.

"Capitalist Baby signs on the X to enter into agreements uniting colleagues to make more money for stockholders."

 is for-

"Yes!" - an affirmative, positive answer to
a question or a challenge.

Yearn - to wish for something with your whole heart.

"Capitalist Baby yearns to say 'Yes, and ...,'
'Yes, here's how ...' 'Yes, we could...' He's an Optimist!"

 is for-

Zeal - energetic willingness to pursue one's world view.

Zero - a number that represents a null
value or no quantity of a thing.

*"Capitalist Baby built the business up from zero money
and zero output. She may return to zero more than once.
Nonetheless, she keeps going with zeal."*